MOHAWK
History and Culture

Helen Dwyer and Sierra Adare

Consultant Robert J. Conley
Sequoyah Distinguished Professor at Western Carolina University

Gareth Stevens
Publishing

Please visit our website, **www.garethstevens.com**. For a free color catalog of all our high-quality books, call toll free 1-800-542-2595 or fax 1-877-542-2596.

Library of Congress Cataloging-in-Publication Data

Dwyer, Helen.
Mohawk history and culture / Helen Dwyer and Sierra Adare.
    p. cm. — (Native American library)
Includes index.
ISBN 978-1-4339-6670-5 (pbk.)
ISBN 978-1-4339-6671-2 (6-pack)
ISBN 978-1-4339-6668-2 (library binding)
1. Mohawk Indians—History. 2. Mohawk Indians—Social life and customs. I. Adare, Sierra. II. Title.
E99.M8D975 2012
974.7004'975542—dc23

                    2011026007

New edition published in 2012 by
Gareth Stevens Publishing
111 East 14th Street, Suite 349
New York, NY 10003

First edition published 2005 by Gareth Stevens Publishing

Copyright © 2012 Gareth Stevens Publishing

Produced by Discovery Books
Project editor: Helen Dwyer
Designer and page production: Sabine Beaupré
Photo researchers: Tom Humphrey and Helen Dwyer
Maps: Stefan Chabluk

Photo credits: Art Directors and Trip Photo Library: p.26; Corbis: pp. 7 Marilyn Angel Wynn/Nativestock Pictures), 17, 22, 27 (both), 31, 35, 38 (Christopher J. Morris), 39 (Fred Thornhill/X02272/Reuters); Native Stock: pp. 10 (bottom), 13, 19, 20, 21 (both), 24, 32, 37; North Wind Picture Archives: pp. 10 (top), 12, 15 (both), 16 (top); Peter Newark's American Pictures: pp. 14, 16 (bottom), 25 (both); Shutterstock: pp. 5 (Duncan Gilbert), 29 (Thomas W. Woodruff), 33 (SF photo); Sierra Adare: p. 34; Tracey Deer: p. 36; Wikimedia: pp. 8, 28 (US FWS).

Printed in the United States of America

CPSIA compliance information: Batch # CW12GS: For further information contact Gareth Stevens, New York, New York at 1-800-542-2595.

CONTENTS

Words that appear in the glossary are printed in **boldface** type the first time they appear in the text.

INTRODUCTION

The Mohawks are a people of New York State in the United States and of Quebec and Ontario in southern Canada. They are just one of the many groups of Native Americans who live today in North America. There are well over five hundred Native American tribes in the United States and more than six hundred in Canada. At least three million people in North America consider themselves to be Native Americans. But who are Native Americans, and how do the Mohawks fit into the history of North America's native peoples?

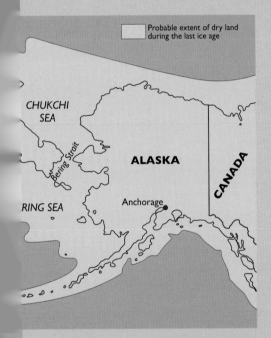

Siberia (Asia) and Alaska (North America) are today separated by an area of ocean named the Bering Strait. During the last ice age, the green area on this map was at times dry land. The Asian ancestors of the Mohawks walked from one continent to the other.

THE FIRST IMMIGRANTS

Native Americans are people whose **ancestors** settled in North America thousands of years ago. These ancestors probably came from eastern parts of Asia. Their **migrations** probably occurred during cold periods called **ice ages**. At these times, sea levels were much lower than they are now. The area between northeastern Asia and Alaska was dry land, so it was possible to walk between the continents.

Scientists are not sure when these migrations took place, but it must have been more than twelve thousand years ago. Around that time, water levels rose and covered the land between Asia and the Americas.

The Cliff Palace at Mesa Verde, Colorado, is the most spectacular example of Native American culture that survives today. It consists of more than 150 rooms and pits built around A.D. 1200 from sandstone blocks.

By around ten thousand years ago, the climate had warmed and was similar to conditions today. The first peoples in North America moved around the continent in small groups, hunting wild animals and collecting a wide variety of plant foods. Gradually these groups spread out and lost contact with each other. They developed separate **cultures** and adopted lifestyles that suited their **environments.**

SETTLING DOWN

Although many tribes continued to gather food and hunt or fish, some Native Americans began to live in settlements and grow crops. Their homes ranged from underground pit houses and huts of mud and thatch to dwellings in cliffs. By 3500 B.C., a plentiful supply of fish in the Pacific Ocean and in rivers had enabled people to settle in large coastal villages from Alaska to Washington State. In the deserts of Arizona more than two thousand years later, farmers constructed hundreds of miles of **irrigation** canals to carry water to their crops.

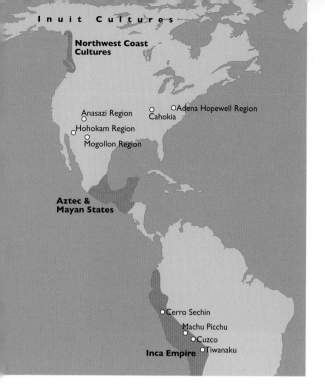

Northwest Coast
Cultures

Anasazi Region
Hohokam Region
Mogollon Region

Adena Hopewell Region
Cahokia

Aztec &
Mayan States

Cerro Sechin
Machu Picchu
Cuzco
Inca Empire Tiwanaku

This map highlights some of the main early Native American cultures.

In the Ohio River valley between 700 B.C. and A.D. 500, people of the Adena and Hopewell cultures built clusters of large burial mounds, such as the Serpent Mound in Ohio, which survives today. In the Mississippi **floodplains**, the native peoples formed complex societies. They created mud and thatch temples on top of flat earth pyramids. Their largest town, Cahokia, in Illinois, contained more than one hundred mounds and may have been home to thirty thousand people.

At some point, the ancestors of the Mohawks arrived in the present-day region of New York State and southern Canada. They lived in villages consisting of longhouses, each of which sheltered several families. They survived by farming, hunting, and fishing. Before A.D. 1600, possibly as early as the twelfth century, the Mohawks joined with four other tribes, who spoke similar Iroquoian languages, to establish the Haudenosaunee, or Iroquois, **Confederacy**.

CONTACT WITH EUROPEANS

Around A.D. 1500, European ships reached North America. The first explorers were the Spanish. Armed with guns and riding horses, they took over land and forced the Native Americans to work for them. The Spanish were followed by the British, Dutch, and French, who were looking for land to settle and for opportunities to trade. The Mohawks made agreements with the Dutch in 1609 and the British in 1664, in which each group recognized the other as an equal nation.

A recreation of a traditional Iroquois village with several longhouses, located in New York State.

However, when Native Americans met Europeans they came into contact with diseases, such as smallpox and measles, that they had never experienced before. At least one half of all Native Americans, and possibly many more than that, were unable to overcome these diseases and died.

Guns were also disastrous for Native Americans. At first, only the Europeans had guns, which enabled them to overcome native peoples in fights and battles. Eventually, Native American groups obtained guns and used them in conflicts with each other.

Horses, too, had a big influence in Native American lifestyles, especially on the Great Plains. Some groups became horse breeders and traders. People were able to travel greater distances and began to hunt buffalo on horseback. Soon horses became central to Plains trade and social life.

Native American groups were also forced to take sides and fight in wars between the French and British. The Mohawks usually sided with the British against the French, because the French supported the Mohawks' traditional enemies, the Algonquians. With Mohawk help, the British drove the French out of large areas of North America. During the American Revolution, the Mohawks supported the British. They were defeated, and many Mohawks fled to Canada to live on land given to them by the British.

At the end of the 1700s, people of European descent began to migrate over the Appalachian Mountains, looking for new land to farm and exploit. By the middle of the nineteenth century, they had reached the west coast of North America. This expansion was disastrous for Native Americans.

RESERVATION LIFE

Many native peoples were pressured into moving onto **reservations** to the west. The biggest of these reservations later became the U.S. state of Oklahoma. Native Americans who tried to remain in their homelands were attacked and defeated. The Mohawks were forced to resettle on reservations in the United States and Canada.

New laws in the United States and Canada took away most of the control Native Americans had over their lives. They were expected to give up their cultures and adopt the ways and habits of white Americans. It became a crime to practice their traditional religions. Children were taken from their homes and placed in **boarding schools**, where they were forbidden to speak their native languages.

An 1882 portrait of the last surviving Haudenosaunee Confederacy warriors who fought on the side of the British in 1812. On the left is Mohawk chief Smoke Johnson, or Sakayengwaraton (1792–1886).

Despite this **persecution**, many Native Americans clung on to their cultures through the first half of the twentieth century. The Society of American Indians was founded in 1911 and its campaign for U.S. citizenship for Native Americans was successful in 1924. Other Native American organizations were formed to promote traditional cultures and to campaign politically for Native American rights.

THE ROAD TO SELF-GOVERNMENT

Despite these campaigns, Native Americans on reservations endured **poverty** and very low standards of living. Many of them moved away to work and live in cities, where they hoped life would be better. In most cases, they found life just as difficult. They not only faced **discrimination** and **prejudice** but also could not compete successfully for jobs against more established ethnic groups.

In the 1970s, the American Indian Movement (AIM) organized large protests that attracted attention worldwide. They highlighted the problems of unemployment, discrimination, and poverty that Native Americans experienced in North America.

The AIM protests led to changes in policy. Some new laws protected the civil rights of Native Americans, while other laws allowed tribal governments to be formed. Today tribal governments have a wide range of powers. They operate large businesses and run their own schools and health care.

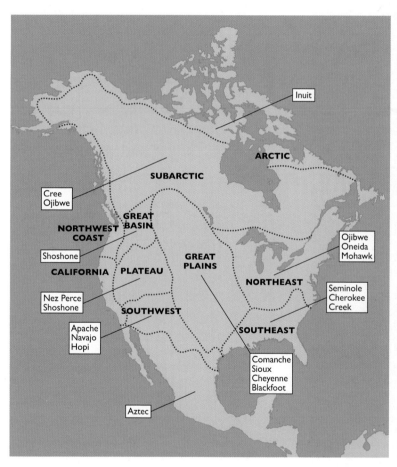

This map of North America highlights the main Native American cultural groups, along with the smaller groups, or tribes, featured in this series of books.

LAND AND ORIGINS

LAND OF THE MOHAWKS

The Mohawk people live mostly in northern New York State and across the border in Canada; they number around twenty-five thousand. The Mohawks call themselves *Kanien'kehake*, which means "People of the Flint" because of the flint **quarries** in the eastern part of their territory. *Mohawk* means "cowards" in the language of the Abenaki Indians, traditional enemies and neighbors of the Mohawks. Although the Mohawks were considered powerful warriors, the Dutch and British traders soon used the Abenaki term Mohawk because it was easier to pronounce.

ORIGIN STORIES

No one knows for sure how Mohawks and other Native Americans came to North America, but for centuries, most native cultures have told stories about their origins.

Though he probably never saw an Indian, an eighteenth-century artist drew this Mohawk man's clothing correctly. However, he added an incorrect bow and feather. Also, Mohawks never wore bones in their noses.

The turtle (right) symbolizes Earth. On her back is the white pine Tree of Peace.

Long ago, according to a traditional Mohawk story, people lived in the Sky World. One day, a hole opened up at the base of a great tree. Sky Woman fell through it toward the sea, which completely covered Earth. A group of blue herons caught her. She then lived on the back of a great sea turtle floating on the water. There, she gave birth to a daughter, who had twin boys. Soon many people lived on Turtle Island, the Mohawks' name for Earth.

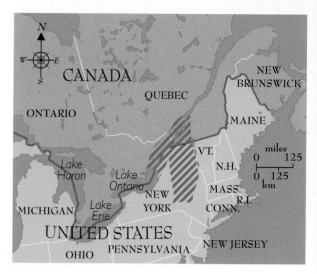

The Mohawks' original homelands stretched through today's New York State and areas of Quebec and Ontario.

Mohawk elders also tell of the people coming from the American Southwest. According to this belief, thousands of years before history was written down, the Mohawks slowly moved into what is now the northeastern United States. Their homelands extended from modern central New York State up into Canada.

The Mohawk Language

Mohawk is an **oral** language. It was not written down until priests came to **convert** Mohawks to Christianity. The priests believed the Mohawks were not smart enough to understand more than twelve letters of the English alphabet so the Mohawk written language uses only twelve letters.

Mohawk	Pronunciation	English
sekoh	say-go	hello
yoh	yo	so long
hen'en	ha-a	yes
yah	e-yah	no
yeksa' ah	yek-saw	girl
raksa' ha	lock-saw	boy

HISTORY

MOHAWKS FORM THE HAUDENOSAUNEE CONFEDERACY

The people in the Iroquoian language groups, which include the Mohawks, refer to themselves as Haudenosaunee, meaning "the people building a longhouse." This large wood and bark structure housed families of the same **clan**. The word "longhouse" not only describes Haudenosaunee multifamily homes, but also the multination league, the Haudenosaunee Confederacy, the Mohawks founded.

A village was made up of several longhouses with a fence made of long stakes surrounding them.

A MESSAGE OF PEACE

Centuries before the arrival of the Europeans, Mohawks often fought against four other Haudenosaunee nations — the Oneida, Cayuga, Seneca, and Onondaga. Then came a man known as Skennenrahawi, or the Peacemaker, a man of great vision. He knew the only way the Haudenosaunee nations could stand up to their common enemy, the Algonquians, was to unite. He also knew the nations respected the brave Mohawk warriors. If the Mohawks agreed to peace, the others would, too.

As the first to accept the Peacemaker's Great Law of Peace, the Mohawks are the "older brother" in the Haudenosaunee Confederacy. The Oneidas, Cayugas, and Senecas soon joined, but the Onondagas delayed until their leader was convinced of the wisdom of the Great Law. In 1722, a southeastern tribe, the Tuscaroras, joined, making it the Confederacy of Six Nations. The French called the Confederacy and its members the "Iroquois"; Mohawks prefer their own word, "Haudenosaunee."

EARLY CONTACT WITH EUROPEANS

Living in villages between what is now Albany, New York, and Quebec in Canada, the Mohawk people were the farthest east of all the Haudenosaunee Confederacy. Thus, they were the first in the Confederacy to come into contact with the Europeans arriving

Aiionwatha and Wampum Belts

An Onondagan, Aiionwatha made the first **wampum belt** by stringing together purple and white shell beads. Their design represented the parts of the Great Law of Peace, a system of rules for behavior between individuals and groups. Aiionwatha used the belt to teach the Mohawks and other Haudenosaunees the Great Law. Called *Anakoha*, wampum belts are sacred to the Mohawks.

This wampum belt fragment recounts the historic forming of the Haudenosaunee Confederacy. The squares stand for four of the original five nations linked with the Tree of Peace.

in North America, meeting the French in 1534, the Dutch in 1609, and the English in 1664.

During the late 1500s, the Mohawks were at war with the Algonquians, who wanted to expand their territory. In exchange for furs, the French traded weapons to the Algonquians. Thus the Mohawks welcomed Dutch traders and the guns they supplied for the native war. In 1613, the Mohawks and the Dutch formed an **alliance** and agreed to a **treaty**. This treaty, the first between Mohawks and Europeans, was called the Covenant Chain and was recorded on the Two-Row Wampum Belt. The rows ran next to each other the length of the belt. This pattern meant each nation would recognize and honor the other as an independent and equal nation. In 1664, the Dutch handed over control of the lands they had settled on in North America to the English, who renewed the Covenant Chain with the Mohawks.

TEONIAHIGARAWE AND THE BRITISH

Mohawk leader Teoniahigarawe, called Hendricks by Europeans, met with British governor George Clinton in New York in 1753. Ignoring treaties, Clinton had broken the Covenant Chain by allowing more British settlers to move onto Mohawk land. When Clinton refused to honor the Covenant Chain and remove the settlers, Teoniahigarawe told him, "My heart aches because we Mohawks have always been faithful to you. . . . The covenant chain is broken."

Teoniahigarawe posed in European-style dress for this formal portrait by Dutch painter John Verelst while visiting Queen Anne in England in 1710.

Sir William Johnson, the trader and soldier who lived among the Mohawks, married a Mohawk woman whom the British called Molly Brant. Her Mohawk name is unknown.

The British Empire, preparing to wage war against France over territory in Europe and North America, sent Sir William Johnson to settle its differences with Teoniahigarawe. Johnson persuaded Teoniahigarawe to renew the Covenant Chain. The British did not, however, keep their part of the Covenant Chain agreement; settlers continued to take Mohawk land.

The Mohawks gave the British their first victory in what became known as the French and Indian War (1754–63) at the Battle of Lake George in 1755, where Teoniahigarawe died. With the help of the Mohawks and other native nations, the British pushed the French out of much of North America.

Produced in 1771, this map shows the locations of the independent nations of the Haudenosaunees in what is currently New York State and Canada.

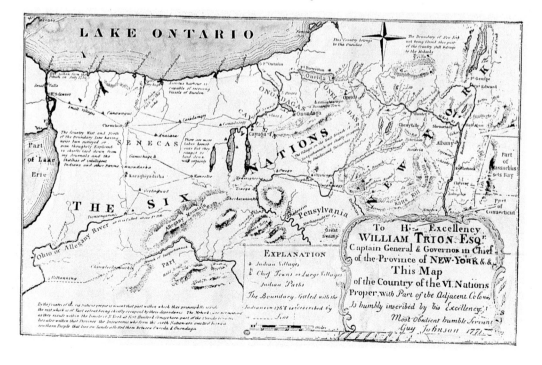

Thayendanegea, also known as Joseph Brant, fought for the British during the American Revolution and acted as translator between the British and the Mohawks.

MOHAWKS IN THE AMERICAN REVOLUTION

The American Revolution divided the Haudenosaunee Confederacy into those who fought for the British and those who fought for the Americans. Sir William Johnson's Mohawk brother-in-law, Joseph Brant, persuaded four of the nations to side with the British, including the Mohawks.

In 1778, Brant's forces defeated American troops. Wanting to crush the native forces, General George Washington ordered that all Haudenosaunees, including those allied with the Americans, should not "merely be overrun but destroyed." Within a year, Mohawk territory in today's New York State was destroyed, laid to waste by General John Sullivan's "scorched-earth" policy. His troops burned villages, corn fields, fruit orchards — everything — to the ground. They killed every man, woman, and child they could find. More starved to death that winter.

U.S. General John Sullivan led soldiers in a number of battles against both the British and Native Americans during the American Revolution.

16

The 1783 Treaty of Paris signed by the Americans and British ended the American Revolution. It also set up the U.S.–Canadian border through Mohawk country.

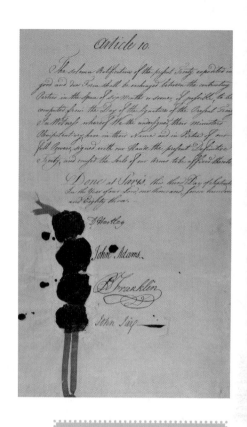

IN CANADA AND THE UNITED STATES

At the end of the war in 1783 when the colonies became the United States, many Mohawks followed Brant into British-held Canada. The government gave 1,200 square miles (3,100 square kilometers) of land on the Grand River in Ontario to Brant in 1784 to "take possession of and . . . enjoy forever." As members of all Haudenosaunee nations fled the United States, Grand River became the center of the Canadian side of the Haudenosaunee Confederacy. There have been two separate Confederacies ever since.

Mohawks who remained in their Mohawk Valley homeland signed a treaty with the United States at Fort Stanwix in 1784 that clearly defined the boundaries of the Mohawks' land. Mohawks never surrendered their homelands and did not give up their right to define themselves as a separate nation or to run their own lives with their own traditional form of government.

MOHAWKS FORCED TO MOVE

After the American Revolution, most Mohawks were forced to resettle around Akwesasne — today a reservation in northern New York State

The Indians live much better than most of the Mohawk River farmers, their Houses very well furnished with all necessary Household utensils, great plenty of Grain, several Horses, cows and waggons (sic). . . . The town . . . consisted of [128] houses, mostly very large and elegant.

U.S. General John Sullivan's officers and men praising the wealth of the Mohawk towns they were destroying

and Ontario and Quebec, Canada — or in other locations in Canada. The 1783 Treaty of Paris set the boundary between Canada and the United States, drawing it right through Mohawk territory.

The War of 1812 continued the fight between the British and the Americans. As in the American Revolution, the British wanted Mohawks to fight as their ally. However, the Mohawks remained **neutral** until the American and British forces fought a battle on Mohawk lands at Akwesasne. Defending their lands forced the Mohawks into the war, again splitting the people between those who fought for the Americans and those who fought for the British.

During the mid-1800s, New York State unsuccessfully tried to get the U.S. government to move the Mohawks to Indian Territory (present-day Oklahoma) west of the Mississippi River. The Canadians, however, did succeed in seizing Mohawk land along the Grand River in Canada and refused to return it to the Mohawks. Eventually, both the Canadian and U.S. governments passed laws that forced Mohawks off their traditional lands and onto reservations.

Children Taken from Their Families

On both sides of the United States–Canadian border, whites stole Mohawk children from the reservations and sent them far away to boarding schools. At these schools, children were not allowed to speak the Mohawk language, wear their own clothes, or follow their own religion. They were mistreated, and many died. Others ran away.

THE TWENTIETH CENTURY

During the early and mid-1900s, the U.S. and Canadian governments continued their policies from the 1700s. They denied the Mohawks their right as an independent nation to practice their traditional government, religious beliefs, and customs. The governments also refused to allow Mohawk women the right to vote

This modern Mohawk man wears the traditional clothing of his people, celebrating and helping to educate others about his culture.

in tribal affairs. The Mohawks, however, continued to practice their traditions in secret.

By the late 1900s, Mohawks and other Haudenosaunees began to openly practice their traditional form of government, religious beliefs, and customs despite objections from the U.S. and Canadian governments. Mohawk women now publicly help form the traditional government, participate in religious ceremonies, and teach Mohawk customs, history, and beliefs to children. Today, members of the Haudenosaunee (Iroquois) nations have their own passports and have appeared before the United Nations representing independent nations, despite the objections of the U.S. and Canadian governments.

Democracy in Action?

In 1885, the Canadian government forced its own version of tribal leadership on the Mohawks. First, it declared the traditional Mohawk government to be illegal and put the traditionally elected Mohawk leaders of Akwesasne in prison. The Canadians then picked fifteen other Mohawks, got them drunk, and then forced them to choose as leaders Akwesasne residents whom the Canadian government believed would do whatever it told them to do. As one Akwesasne sachem, or leader, Michael Mitchell, described the Canadians' conduct in 1989, "This is the way Canada introduced our people to the principles of their **democracy**."

TRADITIONAL WAY OF LIFE

Longhouses were windproof, and their roofs resisted rain, ice, and snow. Shelves for storage lined the interior.

MOHAWK HOME LIFE

Traditionally, Mohawks lived in villages consisting of several longhouses made of elm bark covering poles bent in an upside-down U shape. The longhouses were usually 20 feet (6 meters) wide and 150 feet (46 m) long. Several families lived in a single longhouse.

Mohawks are matrilineal, which means that all children belong to their mother's clan. They are also matrilocal, which means that after marriage men move to the wife's home. Women control the land, deciding what to plant and where. Traditionally, Mohawk women raised corn, melons, squash, pumpkins, beans, tobacco, sunflowers, and peas. They kept apple orchards and tapped maple trees for syrup and sugar. Girls learned gardening from their mothers and aunts.

Mohawk men traveled throughout their territory, hunting, fishing, and trading with other native nations. Boys learned from their fathers and uncles how to fish, hunt, and clear the land.

Before contact with Europeans, Mohawks dressed in two-piece deerskin garments, leggings, and moccasins embroidered with porcupine quills. Men wore feather headdresses for ceremonies. Later, **broadcloth** clothing replaced deerskin, and trade beads replaced quills. Women wore **pantalets**, overdresses of calico, and blankets like shawls. They also carried beaded pocketbooks.

The beadwork on these Mohawk moccasins is done in a traditional design using modern beads. The original trade beads were darker.

Tewaarathon: A Spiritual Practice

In traditional Mohawk culture, playing the game of *Tewaarathon* is a way of thanking the Creator, who gave the game to the Mohawks, for the gifts of life to all things on Mother Earth. During the late eighteenth century, whites, who believed it was a war game, discouraged the Mohawks from playing Tewaarathon. But, in fact, Mohawks have never stopped playing the game.

The size of the field depends on the number of players. Traditionally, two teams, each numbering from five to one thousand people, played on a field that could be between 100 yards (91 m) and 2 miles (3 km) long. Historically and in modern times, players throw or carry a ball to their goal at the far end of the field using sticks with nets.

Named *lacrosse* by nonnatives, Tewaarathon is played by children and adults of all ages.

Both the Thanksgiving Address and the Code of Handsome Lake stress the Mohawks' sense of responsibility for taking good care of the land and all its beauties.

BELIEFS

At the core of Mohawk belief is the Creator, who shares power with others — trees, plants, animals, water, other spirits, and people — who are often messengers for the Creator. The Mohawks give thanks to the Creator and all living things through the Thanksgiving Address, which dates back to the origins of the Haudenosaunees and is not related to U.S. or Canadian Thanksgiving holidays. According to tradition, Sky Woman's son, the Good-Minded Twin, began this method of offering thanks for all of creation. The Address has always been and continues to be spoken at the beginning and closing of all ceremonies and governmental meetings.

The Address has fifteen or sixteen sections and reminds all Haudenosaunees how they are connected to everything in the universe. Each section starts by naming the things Creator has provided, such as the earth, animals, birds, and bodies of water, and describing their purpose, duties, and responsibilities and how they are connected with all living things. For example, the

Creator created many varieties of meadow grasses that grow every spring and bring pleasure to all people, including children. Grasses also bring happiness to the animals that eat the grasses and the birds that use the grasses to build their nests. People are reminded throughout every section to be grateful and offer thanks. All sections end with "So it will be in our minds."

In 1799, a Seneca man named Skaniateriio (or Handsome Lake) received visions from the Creator in the form of four messengers. The messengers brought Handsome Lake a new code for living for the Haudenosaunee people. The code contained 130 messages, stories, songs, ceremonies, and addresses to be used with the Thanksgiving Address. This code, called the *Gaiwiio*, or the "Great Good Message," stresses the importance of maintaining strong traditional families, honoring tribal ways, and caring for the land. Besides upholding old ways, the code provided help in adjusting to the changes forced on the Haudenosaunees after the American Revolution.

Commonly called the Longhouse Religion, the Code of Handsome Lake is currently practiced by many Mohawks. Every autumn, people go to their local community's longhouse, on or off the reservation, for three days to hear the Code.

The Code of Handsome Lake

The Code tells the people how to continue ceremonies that renew both individuals and the community. It teaches how and why to give thanksgiving when planting food, how to care for the land, and how to adjust to living on the smaller plots on reservations. The Code discourages drinking and gambling and advises Mohawk parents on how to raise a family that will help the community. It also recounts Handsome Lake's journey to the Creator's land and teaches historical events.

TRADITIONAL GOVERNMENT

The Mohawk Nation has three clans — Turtle, Wolf, and Bear. Traditionally, the oldest woman becomes the Clan Mother, the head of the clan. The Clan Mother selects the leader, the peacekeeper, and the **faithkeeper** for her clan. These men are called sachems rather than chiefs. Once the clan approves the Clan Mother's choices, the sachems form the leadership of the Mohawk Nation.

These leaders, or sachems, also become part of the *rotiiane*, the Grand Council of the Haudenosaunee Confederacy, made up of fifty leaders from the Six Nations. These leaders serve for life unless they are "dehorned" (removed from office) by the Clan Mothers.

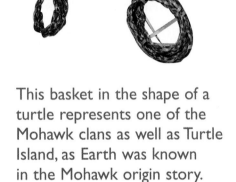

This basket in the shape of a turtle represents one of the Mohawk clans as well as Turtle Island, as Earth was known in the Mohawk origin story.

How Clan Mothers Choose Leaders

Clan Mothers watch male children from birth through manhood to determine who will make good leaders. They select men for leadership positions based on four rules: A man must be married with at least one child. He must have committed no crime. He must not have expressed a desire to become a leader. He must not have shown any improper behavior, especially toward women.

Honeeyeathtawnorow, from the Wolf clan, met with Queen Anne. He is shown here in European-style clothing. The dog at his feet is Dutch artist John Verelst's idea of what a North American wolf looked like.

Sagayeathquapiethtow, member of the Bear clan, was a Mohawk leader who also met with Queen Anne. He wears a European-style **toga** and cape. The London *Daily Courant* newspaper stated that his tattoos were more impressive than scary.

The Grand Council passes all laws for the Six Nations. All fifty leaders must agree on every law, a concept called governing by **consensus**. The Haudenosaunees call this kind of governing "one heart, one mind, one head, and one body" for the peace and power of the Six Nations. Unfortunately, historically and in more recent years, both the U.S. and Canadian governments have tried to force the Mohawks to give up their traditional form of government.

The Great Law of Peace still guides all traditional members of the Haudenosaunee Confederacy as they go about their daily lives. Passed down from grandparents to grandchildren, this guideline tells each person how to behave toward others. The basic principles of the Great Law of Peace are good behavior toward each other, good behavior within the Confederacy, positive **spiritual** beliefs, and a positive attitude toward all other forms of life.

RESERVATION LIFE

Almost from their arrival, Europeans forced Mohawks to **assimilate** to white culture by wearing European-style clothing and practicing European customs, laws, languages, and religion. Children who went to church-run schools at Akwesasne and on other reservations were punished for speaking Mohawk or practicing the Longhouse Religion. They were also discouraged from playing Tewaarathon (lacrosse). Mohawk children were taught only Euro-American history and languages.

Today Mohawk children are learning their language again. This sign — "Our children's future, everyone's responsibility" — appears on the Kahnawake Indian Reserve, a Mohawk reservation near Montreal in Canada.

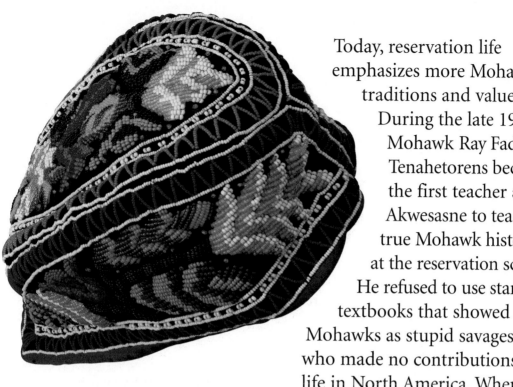

Today, reservation life emphasizes more Mohawk traditions and values. During the late 1900s, Mohawk Ray Fadden-Tenahetorens became the first teacher at Akwesasne to teach true Mohawk history at the reservation school. He refused to use standard textbooks that showed Mohawks as stupid savages who made no contributions to life in North America. When he retired, he built the Six Nations Museum in Onchiota, New York.

This Mohawk hat (top) beaded with a floral design and Haudenosaunee vessel from around 1500 are both displayed at the Six Nations Museum.

Mohawk Views of Reservations

If only we were left alone, we could redevelop our society . . . which was old in democracy when Europe knew only **monarchs**.
Ernest Benedict (Mohawk), 1941

No nation has the right to hold a captive nation.
Mohawk Warrior Society, 1981

Haudenosaunee Symbols

For the peoples of the Haudenosaunee Confederacy, a bundle of five arrows represents each of the five original nations, while the circle represents the cycle of life and the unity of the nations.

Another of the most important Haudenosaunee symbols is the Pine Tree that represents the Great Law of Peace. It has four great roots that point north, south, east, and west.

The white pine is a tall tree of northeastern North America. In the time when the Haudenosaunee Confederacy was created, white pines covered large areas of the continent. The needles grow in bundles of five, so they are another symbol of the Haudenosaunee nations.

At the top of the Pine Tree sits an Eagle, which keeps watch for any approaching threats to the Haudenosaunee peoples. The Eagle is also thought to be a messenger sent by the Creator. The following story explains its origin.

THE COMING OF THE EAGLE

Once, soon after humans were created, a boy was born, and the elders prayed to the spirit world for a name for him. The name they received surprised everyone. He was to be called He Who Walks a Different Path.

And so the boy was different than the other children. He talked to all

The eagle of this story also represents truth and freedom. Today, the golden eagle, like the bald eagle, is protected in the United States.

the animals and birds and refused to hunt them. In return they all became his friends. When the people of his village became angry with him, He Who Walks a Different Path always said that the Creator had given him a different vision.

Eventually he was forced to leave his village and he went to live among his animal friends. Whenever hunters came near, he warned the animals to run away.

When it was time for He Who Walks a Different Path to become a man, strange and frightening things began to happen. His nails became talons, and his hand and arms grew feathers. Then the Creator appeared and told He Who Walks a Different Path that he was to become the Eagle, the carrier of prayers between the people and the Creator.

And so today, the Eagle soars high above the world in Father Sky and sees with the keen eyes of the Creator. When people see the Eagle they are reminded of the closeness of the spirit world.

MOHAWK LIFE TODAY

THE CONTEMPORARY MOHAWKS

Today, over 25,000 Mohawks live on and off reservations all over the United States and Canada, 80 percent of them within Canada, where there are three reservations — Kahnawake, Kanehsatake, and Akwesasne, which straddles the U.S.– Canadian border.

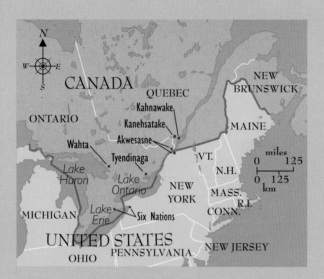

Varying in size, Mohawk reservations are scattered along the eastern border of the United States and Canada.

AKWESASNE

Akwesasne, the only reservation in the United States, is the biggest, with a total of 22,230 acres (9,000 ha). Around 12,000 Mohawks live in Akwesasne, approximately 40 percent of them on the U.S. side and 60 percent on the Canadian side.

Akwesasne has three internal Mohawk governments: The United States forced one government on the Mohawks (the St. Regis Tribal Council); Canada forced a second one (the Mohawk Council of Akwesasne); and the Mohawks chose their own traditional government. Struggles for power between the Canadian and U.S. federal governmental systems have created problems for the Mohawk people.

For example, in Akwesasne, the St. Regis Tribal Council has allowed the opening of **casinos**, which the traditional government opposes. Many Mohawks live by the Great Law of Peace and do not accept casinos, seeing them as bad for both individuals and the community. Others see the casinos as a source of jobs and income in an area that needs both.

In 1974, some Mohawks from Akwesasne occupied land near Altona in New York State. They named their independent community Ganienkeh, and today it still promotes traditional Mohawk values and lifestyles and rejects drugs and alcohol.

Mohawk Sky Walkers

The original "sky walkers," Mohawk high-steel construction workers in New York City.

One Mohawk occupation dates back to the 1880s, when Americans built a bridge across the St. Lawrence River on Mohawk land. As white men worked high up on the narrow beams, Mohawk men and youths would follow them up the beams to watch as they riveted the bridge together. Men willing to work many hundreds of feet above the ground were rare, so bridge engineers taught the Mohawks to work in high-steel construction.

By the 1920s, Mohawks were routinely braving heights. In 1955, Mohawks placed a 222-foot (68-m) television tower on top of the 1,470-foot (450-m) Empire State Building in New York City.

MOHAWK COMMUNITIES IN CANADA

Nearly 8,000 Mohawks live on the 12,500 acres (5,060 ha) of the Kahnawake reservation, on the southern shores of the Saint Lawrence River near Montreal. The tribal council does not allow non-Mohawks to live on its land, and any Mohawk who marries a non-Mohawk must leave.

Most people speak English. Only 10 percent still speak the Mohawk language. Since 1988, Kahnawake has had an immersion school, where children are taught in Mohawk. The tribal council hopes this will keep the language alive among younger people.

One of the most successful Kahnawake businesses is Mohawk Internet Technologies, which provides employment for many local people.

The Kanehsatake reservation, near Oka, Quebec, has about 1,700 Mohawks living on 2,370 acres (960 ha). Tobacco sales are a large part of the tribe's income. More than thirty stores sell tobacco, some of which is produced in Akwesasne and Kahnawake.

Today, some Mohawks make their living by producing **sweetgrass** and wooden baskets such as these, beadwork, or handmade snowshoes.

The Mohawk Chapel in Brantford, Ontario, was built in 1785 by the British for the Mohawks who had fought for Britain in the American Revolution and lost their homelands in New York State. These Mohawks were given land at Brantford, as well as two mills, a school, and the chapel.

The community of Wahta in Muskoka, Ontario, was founded in 1881. Located in a region of forests and lakes, it now owns and runs Ontario's largest cranberry farm.

Tyendinaga Mohawk Territory is the home of the Mohawks of the Bay of Quinte in southeastern Ontario. In 1985, the Tyendinaga Mohawk Council helped set up the First Nations Technical Institute (FNTI) to offer native people post-secondary education. The FNTI provides around sixty jobs in the Quinte area.

The Six Nations of the Grand River is the largest of the First Nations of Canada, located near Brantford, Ontario. It includes people of all the nations in the Haudenosaunee Confederacy, including the Mohawks.

OLD AND NEW

Whether they live on or off the reservation, Mohawks today drive cars; go to school; work in offices, in factories, or on farms; attend universities, and speak English or French. They also participate in Longhouse religious ceremonies, play Tewaarathon for traditional reasons, and speak Mohawk.

Tom Porter and Kanatsiohareke

In 1993, a group of Mohawks headed by elder Tom Porter purchased a 377-acre (153-ha) farm in the Mohawk Valley. There they have reestablished a traditional community on land called Kanatsiohareke. Five to ten families live on the farm at any given time. They grow traditional foods, speak Mohawk, and observe traditional ceremonies.

At Kanatsiohareke, community members use both traditional ways and modern technology to live in harmony with the land; for example, they farm with horses as well as with a tractor. A spring supplies the farm's water and runs the **hydroelectric power** generator. In addition to making traditional crafts, they run a T-shirt shop and a bed-and-breakfast.

"To live in harmony with the Creator, we must live in harmony with nature," explains Porter. "We farm like my grandpa farmed and the generations who came before him."

Kanatsiohareke, "the place of the clean pot," is a traditional community in the heart of the Mohawk Valley, the traditional land of the Mohawks.

AUTHORS, ARTISTS, AND ACTORS

Many Mohawk children have grown up to become successful authors, artists, and actors. Doug George-Kanentiio grew up on the Akwesasne reservation. Since his school days, he has written about important Mohawk issues for newspapers. He **edited** the *Akwesasne Notes* news journal for six years. He also **negotiated** for the Mohawk Nation to get the U.S. government to live up to its treaty agreements.

Artist Bill Powless draws cartoons for the Six Nations of the Grand River reservation newspaper *Tekawennake* in Ontario, Canada. He uses a character that acts like Tonto, a character in the 1950s *Lone Ranger* television series, to address local issues from both serious and funny viewpoints.

Although portrayed as little more than a **sidekick** and servant to the Lone Ranger, Tonto is a popular figure on Mohawk reservations. The actor who played Tonto on TV and in movies was Mohawk Jay Silverheels, who grew up on the Six Nations reservation.

Mohawk actor Jay Silverheels (right) founded the Indian Actors Workshop in Hollywood to help more Native Americans find roles and change the movie image of Indians.

FILM AND PHOTOGRAPHY

Tracey Deer has directed several films for Rezolution Pictures, a film and television production company owned by Native Americans.

Tracey Deer is a film writer, director, and producer from the Kahnawake reservation. She has made several nonfiction films about Mohawk life that have won many awards. In 2006, she formed her own company, Mohawk Princess productions. *Mohawk Girls* (2005) is about three Mohawk teenagers as well as herself as a teenager.

Photographer Shelley Niro also uses Hollywood images to poke fun at the "Indian princess" image. In her photograph *Final Frontier, First Frame, 1992,* she dressed like a member of TV's *Star Trek* crew. She learned the art of photography by taking photos of her mother and sisters in the attic of the family's home. Niro wanted to show the strength of Mohawk women, Mohawk pride in being Native American, and the fact that Mohawks could have fun, too.

All of my work to date has dealt with native issues because that is what I feel passionate about. Our stories and our communities have so much vibrancy to offer and I'm very committed to expressing that on the big and small screen.

Tracey Deer, director and producer

In the 1990s, Shelley Niro began to make films and videos. The first was *It Starts With a Whisper*, in which a young woman explores her identity and cultural background. *Honey Moccasin* is a comedy thriller set on a reservation. *Kissed by Lightning* is about a Mohawk artist and was inspired by an old Iroquois story.

The Smoke Dance

When the wind shifted and longhouses became smoky, elders would ask the young people to dance the smoke away. Drummers played a fast beat on water drums, while dancers spun and twisted. The movement forced the smoke to rise and escape through the vent in the roof. The best dancers stopped the instant the drum hit its final beat.

This is the origin of the traditional Smoke Dance. Today, Smoke Dancers dressed in traditional Haudenosaunee outfits perform at powwows. Judges watch for dancers staying with the drumbeat and stopping on time with the end of the song.

The Sweetgrass Singers are a group of Mohawk women. They perform their songs in traditional dress.

LAND ISSUES

RECLAIMING THE LAND

The 1784 Six Nations treaty **guaranteed** the original five nations of the Haudenosaunee Confederacy their right to their land in New York State. Claiming the state has refused to keep that treaty agreement, five nations of the original Haudenosaunee Confederacy have taken New York State to court over what has been called land-claims issues. In 1989, the Mohawks asked the judge to force the state to give the Mohawks some **public lands**. They've also asked the state to pay rent for land taken from the Mohawks and for the right to buy land offered for sale to add to their small reservation. Although the courts have still not made a final ruling on the Mohawks' **lawsuit**, some Mohawks are not waiting for the justice system to resolve land-claims issues. In recent years they have taken part in several public protests.

In 1990, the town of Oka in Quebec planned to extend a golf course to cover a pine grove and ancient burial site that were sacred to the Mohawks of Kanehsatake.

Ellen Gabriel (center) was a spokeswoman for the Mohawks at Oka in 1990. In 2004, she became the president of the Quebec Native Women's Association.

Tyendinaga Mohawks closed off a busy railroad line in Deseronto, Ontario, for two days in April 2007 to prevent the building of houses on land they claimed was traditionally theirs.

Armed Mohawks occupied the land and refused to move for 78 days. Eventually the golf course expansion was canceled.

In 2006, people of the Six Nations in Caledonia, Ontario, objected to houses being built on their traditional lands by erecting tents and tepees and setting up roadblocks. The following year, Mohawks of the Tyendinaga Mohawk territory in southeastern Ontario blocked the main street of Deseronto to protest another housing development on disputed land.

As for the survival of the Mohawks and the Haudenosaunee Confederacy, traditional Onondaga sachem Oren Lyons sums it up best: "We will determine what our culture is. . . . We are not going to be put in a museum or accept your **interpretation** of our culture. . . .We will continue our ceremonies. We have the right to exist and that right does not come from you or your government."

TIMELINE

Centuries before Europeans	Skennenrahawi (the Peacemaker) brings the Great Law of Peace to the Mohawks, the first nation in the Haudenosaunee Confederacy; the Oneidas, Cayugas, and Senecas soon joined the Mohawks, followed by the Onondagas.
1534	The Mohawks come into contact with the French for the first time.
1609	The Dutch make first contact with the Mohawks.
1613	Mohawks and the Dutch sign the first treaty between the Mohawks and Europeans, called the Covenant Chain; the Mohawks buy guns from the Dutch to fight the Algonquian tribes.
1653	The Mohawks, along with the other nations in the Haudenosaunee Confederacy, make peace with the French.
1664	Mohawks transfer their alliance from the Dutch to the English, renewing the Covenant Chain.
1722	The Tuscarora tribe joins the Haudenosaunee Confederacy.
1753	Teoniahigarawe (Hendricks) meets with Governor George Clinton in New York; the Covenant Chain is broken, then renewed.
1755	The Battle of Lake George in the French and Indian War; Teoniahigarawe is killed; the British are victorious with the help of the Mohawks.
1779	General John Sullivan destroys Mohawk villages after the Mohawks side with the British in the American Revolution.
1783	Treaty of Paris signed between the United States and Great Britain sets the boundary line between Canada and the United States through the middle of Mohawk territory; many Mohawks move to British-held Canada.
1784	Mohawks who remain in the Mohawk Valley sign a treaty with the United States which defines Mohawk boundaries.

1785	Britain provides land with a school and a chapel in Brantford, Ontario, for Mohawks driven out of New York.
1799	Skaniateriio (Handsome Lake), a Seneca, receives the Great Good Message from the Creator and begins the Longhouse religion.
1812	U.S. and British forces fight a battle on Mohawk lands.
1867	Canada illegally seizes Mohawks' land on the Grand River.
1880s	Mohawks begin working on construction projects hundreds of feet above the ground.
1885	The Canadian government imprisons the elected tribal leaders of Akwesasne and forces other Mohawks to choose leaders who will do as the Canadian government demands.
1892	New York State creates the St. Regis Tribal Council and gives this council the right to rule over U.S. Mohawks.
1984	Gambling for profit begins on the Akwesasne Reservation.
1989	Mohawks submit a proposal to U.S. and New York State authorities for the return of lands illegally taken.
1990	Armed Kanehsatake Mohawks occupy land in Oka, Quebec, to prevent the building of a golf course on sacred land and burial sites.
1993	Tom Porter heads a group of Mohawks who purchase land to reestablish Kanatsiohareke, a traditional community in the Mohawk Valley.
1999	New York moves to have the Mohawks' land claims dismissed.
2003	Wahta Mohawks settle a land claim with the Canadian and Ontario governments; they receive compensation and 8,300 acres (3,300 hectares) of land.
2006	Members of the Six Nations of the Grand River occupy disputed land in Caledonia, Ontario, to prevent houses from being built.
2007	Tyendinaga Mohawks occupy the center of Deseronto, Ontario, to prevent housing being built on disputed land.

GLOSSARY

alliance: an agreement between two groups to work together toward a common goal.

ancestors: people from whom an individual or group is descended.

assimilate: to force one group to adopt the culture — the language, lifestyle, and values — of another.

boarding schools: places where students must live at the school.

broadcloth: a thick cloth woven from wool.

casinos: buildings that have slot machines, card games, and other gambling games.

clan: a group of related families.

confederacy: groups of people or nations joined for a common purpose.

consensus: agreement to an opinion or position by all individuals in a group.

convert: to cause a person to change a belief, usually a religious one.

culture: the arts, beliefs, and customs that make up a people's way of life.

democracy: government that is run by the people of a country or their elected representatives, not by a king, queen, or dictator.

discrimination: unjust treatment usually because of a person's race or sex.

edit: arrange and collect written material before publishing it.

elder: a tribal leader.

environment: objects and conditions all around that affect living things and communities.

faithkeeper: a tribal member who provides counsel and guidance for the leader.

floodplain: the area of land beside a river or stream that is covered with water during a flood.

guarantee: to promise that something will happen.

hydroelectric power: electricity generated by moving water.

ice age: a period of time when the earth is very cold and lots of water in the oceans turns to ice.

interpretation: how someone explains something.

irrigation: any system for watering the land to grow plants.

lawsuit: a claim taken to a court of law for a judgment to be made.

migration: movement from one place to another.

monarch: a king, queen, or other ruler of a state or country.

negotiate: to work with others to come to an agreement.

neutral: not supporting any group or groups that oppose each other.

oral: spoken rather than written.

pantalets: long underpants.

persecution: treating someone or a certain group of people badly over a period of time.

poverty: the state of being poor.

prejudice: dislike or injustice that is not based on reason or experience.

public lands: land owned by the state that no one lives on, such as state forest land.

quarry: a place where large amounts of stone or other materials have been cut out of the ground.

reservation: land set aside by the U.S. government for specific Native American tribes to live on.

sidekick: a close companion or friend.

spiritual: affecting the human spirit or religion rather than physical things.

sweetgrass: a grass used widely by the Mohawks and other native peoples for making crafts and for spiritual and trading purposes.

toga: a long piece of cloth wrapped around the body and worn by people in ancient Rome.

treaty: an agreement among nations.

wampum belt: differently colored beads made from shells strung into a belt in unique designs, which serve as reminders of historical events, laws, and treaties.

MORE RESOURCES

WEBSITES:

http://www.bigorrin.org/mohawk_kids.htm
Online Mohawk Indian Fact Sheet For Kids in question-and-answer form with useful links.

http://www.iroquoismuseum.org/
The Learning Longhouse section of the Iroquois Indian Museum website has lots of information about the Haudenosaunee Confederacy as well as the art, music, dance, sports, food, medicine, and beliefs of the peoples of the confederacy.

http://www.mohawkcommunity.com/
The website of the Kanatsiohareke community in the Mohawk Valley, which preserves traditional culture.

http://www.native-languages.org/mohawk.htm
Links to online Mohawk language resources.

http://www.native-languages.org/mohawk-legends.htm
Many links to Mohawk legends and traditional stories and to books on Mohawk mythology.

http://www.nativelynx.qc.ca/en/cineastes/deer.html
A web page about the film director Tracey Deer, including an interview.

http://www.nfb.ca/film/high_steel
A 1965 film about the Mohawks who erected steel skyscraper frames in Manhattan.

http://www.tuscaroras.com/graydeer/pages/childrenspage.htm
A kids' page about historic Mohawk clothing.

http://www.rom.on.ca/digs/longhouse
Information on Haudenosaunee longhouses.

BOOKS:

Carvell, Marlene. *Sweetgrass Basket.* Dutton Juvenile, 2005.

Dolbear, Emily J., and Peter Benoit. *The Iroquois (True Books).* Children's Press, 2011.

Gibson, Karen Bush. *Native American History for Kids: With 21 Activities.* Chicago Review Press, 2010.

Kalman, Bobbie. *Life in a Longhouse Village (Native Nations of North America).* Crabtree Publishing Company, 2001.

King, David C. *First People.* DK Children, 2008.

King, David C. *The Mohawk (First Americans).* Benchmark Books, 2009.

Lomberg, Michelle. *The Iroquois (American Indian Art and Culture).* Chelsea House Publications, 2004.

Murdoch, David S. *North American Indian (DK Eyewitness Books).* DK Children, 2005.

O'Connor, George. *Journey Into Mohawk Country.* First Second, 2006.

Shenandoah, Joanne, and Douglas M. George. *Skywoman: Legends of the Iroquois.* Clear Light Publishers, 2010.

St. Lawrence, Genevieve. *The Iroquois and Their History (We the People).* Compass Point Books, 2005.

Taylor, C. J. *Peace Walker: The Legend of Hiawatha and Tekanawita.* Tundra Books, 2004.

Weitzmann, David. *Skywalkers: Mohawk Ironworkers Build the City.* Flash Point, 2010.

Wilcox, Charlotte. *The Iroquois (Native American Histories).* Lerner Classroom, 2007.

THINGS TO THINK ABOUT AND DO

CONSENSUS VERSUS MAJORITY RULES

In an example of true government by consensus, all fifty leaders of the Grand Council must agree on each law passed. Ask your teacher to explain how this is different from the U.S. idea of democracy and what the difference is between government by consensus and government by majority rule.

HOW TO PICK A LEADER

Clan Mothers follow four basic rules when selecting sachems. (See Chapter Three.) What do you think are the reasons for these rules? Why is a man who has a wife and family a better choice than a single man with no children? Explain your opinions in a paragraph or two.

TRADITIONAL CLOTHING

Go to **http://www.tuscaroras.com/graydeer/pages/paperdolls.htm** and download the paper doll for a traditionally dressed Haudenosaunee man and woman. Carefully cut out the paper dolls and their clothing. Using crayons or colored pencils, color their clothing as described on this web page, which is about traditional Haudenosaunee clothing.

INDEX

TUCKERTON BRANCH
Ocean County Library
380 Bay Avenue
Tuckerton, NJ 08087